Songs After Memory Fractures

poems by

Allyson Jeffredo

Finishing Line Press
Georgetown, Kentucky

Songs After Memory Fractures

Copyright © 2016 by Allyson Jeffredo
ISBN 978-1-63534-049-5 First Edition
All rights reserved under International and Pan-American Copyright Conventions.
No part of this book may be reproduced in any manner whatsoever without written permission from the publisher, except in the case of brief quotations embodied in critical articles and reviews.

ACKNOWLEDGMENTS

Thanks

Julie Paegle, whose endless support is like finding a cool creek during a summer hike. Juan Delgado and the craft his thoughts bring to the multi-facets of life. Bolin Jue and Norah, to your constant busyness and love. Chad Sweeney for putting the twang of harmonica to word. Chance Castro, who is the ether of kindred. Ruben Rodriguez and his ears when I shared the first versions of these poems. Yehsiming Jue for the privilege of using her painting for the cover—a painting I have coveted for many hours.

Publisher: Leah Maines

Editor: Christen Kincaid

Cover Art: Yehsiming Jue

Author Photo: Bolin Jue

Cover Design: Elizabeth Maines

Printed in the USA on acid-free paper.
Order online: www.finishinglinepress.com
also available on amazon.com

Author inquiries and mail orders:
Finishing Line Press
P. O. Box 1626
Georgetown, Kentucky 40324
U. S. A.

Table of Contents

Even Further Than Andromeda or the Owl
i(a). 1
i(b). 2
i(c). 3
ii. 4
iii. 5
iv. 6
v. 7
vi(a). 8
vi(b). 9
vi(c). 10
vi(d). 11
vii. 12
viii. 13
viii(a). 14
viii(b). 15
viiii. 16
x. 17
xi. 18
xii. 19
xiii. 20
xiiii. 21
xv. 22
xvi. 23
xvii. 24
xviii(a). 25
xviii(b). 26
xviiii. 27
xx. 28
xx(a). 29
xx(b). 30
xx(c). 31
xx(d). 32

for dad & papa

Even Further than Andromeda or the Owl

i(a).

you used to be. you shifted from is to was in my sentences so casually
someone   (permanent)   a body
boot prints between door frames   & door frames grass stained
with salt & heat

                                                    to developed

rung on a clothes hanger, strands of film drying in my head
                                          echo
you, an echo underexposed

i(b).

tattered at the edges, a face scrubbed so rough all the ink washed out. eyes perhaps pissed off, smiling. now on light bulbs: iridescent,
                    ill defined in a hive of blurred grains,
a hollow vase. strewn across an ever-shifting sand dune. ventured, difficult, impossible to reventure.

i(c).

us, was us
                        the past is too distant
even further than Andromeda   or the owl   i
hear howling midevenings   & you're gone, i'm
gone   pixels slip between fingers

(____vincible)

a river burning   your already sun   burnt face

                              (in_____)

ii.

sometimes i find memories
in books that have nothing to do
w/ them i'll pick up their edges
& plant them in the garden
hoping one will sprout you i
don't care if you're a redwood
& angry or a sequoia & stuck
in your head as long as i never
find you thirsty w/ shoes untied again

                                        all i want
                                        want all is
                                        is all i want

                                                                 never to lost
                                                                 to find

iii.

    & i ask
where would you be, what would you do?

in the sink pissing. smashing fingers from yesterday's granite.
a calloused deity veined & fixing things like you liked to do
                      sprinklers, my busted eyebrow

i should say like, drop the past tense. you probably still
exist. still. your hourglass in my head trickles

      pixel   by   pixel

until you're no longer a picture. just a name. a place holding
position for someone—not wholly different
                      from a tree—then timbered
into a box (another place holding position) on the shelf
                          (which is not you,
                          though i saw fragments
                          of your uncharred
                          bone)

iv.

    your clothes never left—they used to stand upright in the kitchen
            washing unrinsed dishes: bits of egg & weenie from the
            scratched teflon before the sun met the little san
            bernardino's upset about the mess
            no one's bothered w/ since you left.
no one denounced their gestures. a buoyant animation filled
your shoes at the door, behind the couch, in the driveway.
i would tuck them under the bed (it made little difference)
they would just walk out again.

i figured you were trying to become a tree. plant yourself
somewhere w/ a full trunk of 50 rings, yet to be sunk.
searching for some kind of permanence not found in our
abandoned trampled careful fragile goddamn bodies

v.

we are restless w/ pity
for rain & the interminable
escape of refrigerator hums
        then our tears transparent
        naked on the sheets,
        drawing a fountain for wishes
        dimes without a surface to break
        left exposed & unsorted
        but this was yesterdays ago
        & our tears are no longer
were we always as hologram
as i remember us now?

        gods forbid we grow fainter

                becoming & halted
                my mind trapped mosquitoes
                behind the dark redwood
                every flicker a surrogate for sun
                & i wonder if
                they can even see the sun

vi(a).

because you're gone,
i will be gone too
the last word in your head—
                              EXTINGUISHED
or something more lovely:
the time you rode your first motorcycle
the only hug your father ever gave you

                              maybe it was the future
                              saying go ahead & go
                              days keep spinning
                              quickly skimmed over—
                              the solution for
                              dissolution even doves
                              defunct

vi(b).

still, i imagine you:
stiff, a concrete statue, looking somehow unnatural:

        on your knees,
        chest carved to the sky
        ants crawling your still warm leg

a memory i never saw, yet you're positioned this way

vi(c).

        my mind draws your amness
        to a close, an end point

though there's always that saying:
    when a door closes
    a window shatters
                there's a means
                for escape or
                forgetting

vi(d).

which shadows you
& i have to choose one or the other
     a) you in a green flannel, sweat-ringed hat & muddy boots
     b) you on your knees, a breath left half-inhaled

vii.

the other day was months ago
mouth washed & pristine
in the corner in front of the bookshelf
reminding of things that last
like characters & evolution

viii.

                                  i've lost track of you
                                  & forgot what fresh prints look like
wind washes the pads away
you might be coyote, rabbit
sifting through sand for water, cover

sun washes out your face,
            your body glistens broken
            quartzite reflects
            an SOS for sunlight
            begging to be filled
            not by the sun, but itself
            something real, rough & gritty
            beige & nothing transparent
            except for its weight
            which is weightless like balloons
            ownerless in the desert still
            trying to fly

                            sheets of memory don't give a damn
                            about weight only trajectory

viii(a).

      & the longer they're still

viii(b).

        the least they'll last

viiii.

remind me:
        how do i find water when
        the earth is sanded down?
when clouds are overexposed & shadowless
from too much thought
& recall never re: shows up?

after awhile, i have to pencil
in details an appt. for
tomorrow,

    next sunday,

a month from now

scheduled

      recurring

            'til extinction
or worse
so the world i see now makes sense
                the sky a window / the sky a mirror
w/ yesterday's envelope
pre-postaged & ready to send
when forgetting sets in

x.

if i hold off
until most blanks
need filling, maybe
oh just maybe
those clouds
will cement
secluded from
their naturalness
to disperse

xi.

i want to be water so i can never drown
accountable only for rust & renewal
drains between pavement, channels
anything that hurts to travel: lethargy
or the owl a few weeks damaged
what would the earth look like
inside out eyes impervious to burn
words written in reverse i would be
water nonfragile & so formless
the dogs would sigh me a drop
until i'm all drops & somehow

xii.

           you
        these days
           are laughing
        i thought
          at me
           but the sounds
        too booming
             it seems i can't
         understand
              enough

xiii.

these fragile bodies know what to keep
what to leave behind: hair caught in the drains,
crescents of fingernails freshly shaved,
wet footprints to evaporate upon boiling asphalt

for summer processes every drop
leaves the world full of impressions
of something-seems-missing under the bed
buried in sand it's hard to name like a star pleading
for attention calling and blinking but no one picks up

xiv.

you're the nopal molded from the summer sun
writing our history no one knew would be lost,
loosened like a missed stitch across the gravel
the sun's eaten away but here it's time & age
always desiccating what we forgot could not
be sustained with glue & string & some left
over coffee beans entangled in these words
holds too much meaning off the page time &
age an elusive thing written on your face in
dunes of experiences your wrinkles contain
where it's finally apparent the sand's been
shifting into less steady structures

xv.

i want to keep you
like every grain of sand
we've touched

siphon
fragments
from pockets,
inside
shoes, deep in
bags, under car
floor mats

                        i
                              don't
                know
                          how
                                to
                rebuild
                                    you

xvi.

you drift away neglected in a dandelion's
game into the sunset or owls nest somewhere
that grants wishes for more tenderness than we
can muster

to provide water & sun for each seed & no
longer call yourself a carrier responsible
for holding which opens up in the shade for
new ones to flourish

xvii.

i'm sorry to mention: memory is an escape
master like palm water or lowering
reservoirs, dissolving it trenches itself
further beneath the surface

xviii(a).

& i have to learn goodbye,
that word a knotted muscle needing
work to unwind:

a goodbye rests somewhere between fallen
timber & the owls breast at the cusp
of coveting more to hear than is there
to be said or unsaid or remembered

when goodbye can
is no longer

xviii(b).

these letters are no longer able to shape you
like a file named, saved, but can't be opened
you drift away in the sand wind brushes
off an unused driveway

    fragment by reflection
      reflection by ghost
    ghost by fragment

these letters merely capture a glimpse of you
try to recognize you into a pattern
familiar where you would be froze
        with a smile

your teeth as young & straight as they always were
your hair flipping up between your hat & ears
your face a (permanent) gentle age

xviiii.

memory is a balloon stranded in the desert,
is the leftover warmth after an arm leaves
your shoulders. what it has done can't be
undone and it's around somewhere.

we'll find it in our hair, the gardenia
perfume our moms used to wear & sometimes
it will never resurface tied to a pebble
that skips/ends in the middle of a rockbed
marked with the ring of an evaporated water & we
never stop hoping we'll remember

xx.

in the crisp air of january, the year rewinds.
the rewound inhales a brimming smile like the morning after
a dream all your dead loved ones are alive: sitting
around your grandma's coffee-stained table talking
with crumbs of pan dulce tucked into their laughlines

it's a picture you want to walk into, hang above
your bed, stencil into a rockface and watch as
the stars drink it up

xx(a).

    whatever will hold on the longest,
    wherever I can fish their faces from

xx(b).

the air is too thoughtful, too willing to reshape
memory into the melting snow or the windprint
in the sand. this world is a dream and memory the only
real thing: waning a nascence, nascence a waning

xx(c).

    something to make their smiles solid,
    anything to engrave their stories on

xx(d).

into the morning, memory becomes a deadpan of feathers,
a time magnet for gravity so illustrious until they resemble
the moon dark and refreshing, pressing dew onto your cheeks

here,
two lightnesses meet in a collision of clouds:
a flint of recollection & an arm raised without a story to tell

Allyson Jeffredo has work published in *Badlands, Tin Cannon,* and *Zócalo Public Square*. She is a fellow of The Loft Spoken Word Immersion Fellowship which allows her to teach creative writing and the arts to Elementary School children of the Inland Empire. When she's not writing, one might find her out in the woods playing airsoft.

www.ingramcontent.com/pod-product-compliance
Lightning Source LLC
LaVergne TN
LVHW041603070426
835507LV00011B/1292